THE SKELETAL SYSTEM

EARLY BIRD
BODY SYSTEMS

BY CAROLINE ARNOLD

LERNER PUBLICATIONS COMPANY • MINNEAPOLIS

Lerner Publications Company
A division of Lerner Publishing Group
241 First Avenue North
Minneapolis, MN 55401 U.S.A.

Website address: www.lernerbook.com

Library of Congress Cataloging-in-Publication Data

Arnold, Caroline.
    The skeletal system / by Caroline Arnold.
        p.   cm. — (Early bird body systems)
    Includes index.
    Summary: Explains how the different types of bones of the body work harmoniously together.
    ISBN: 0–8225–5140–3 (lib. bdg. : alk. paper)
    1. Human skeleton—Juvenile literature. [1. Skeleton. 2. Bones.] I. Title. II. Series.
QM101.A75 2005
611'.71—dc22   2003023026

Manufactured in the United States of America
1 2 3 4 5 6 – JR – 10 09 08 07 06 05

CONTENTS

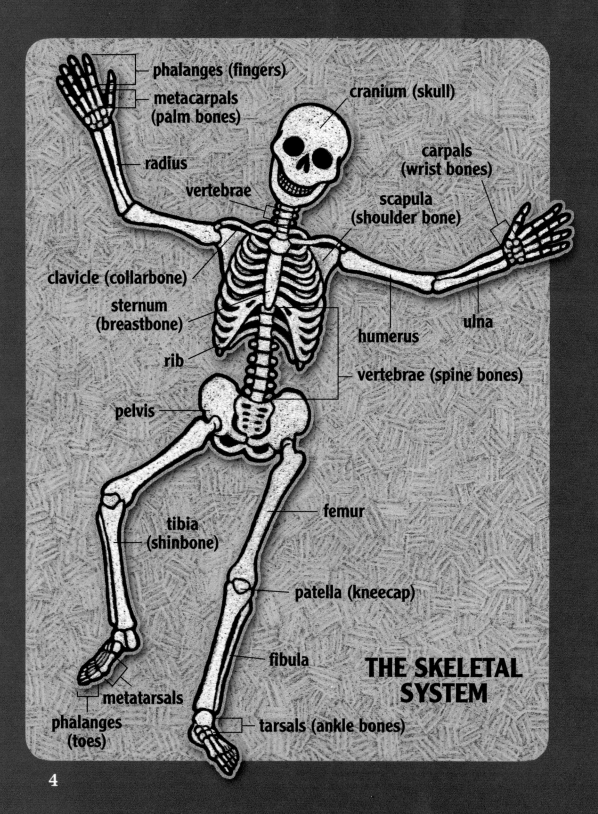

phalanges (fingers)

metacarpals
(palm bones)

cranium (skull)

radius

carpals
(wrist bones)

vertebrae

scapula
(shoulder bone)

clavicle (collarbone)

sternum
(breastbone)

rib

humerus

ulna

vertebrae (spine bones)

pelvis

femur

tibia
(shinbone)

patella (kneecap)

fibula

THE SKELETAL
SYSTEM

metatarsals

phalanges
(toes)

tarsals (ankle bones)

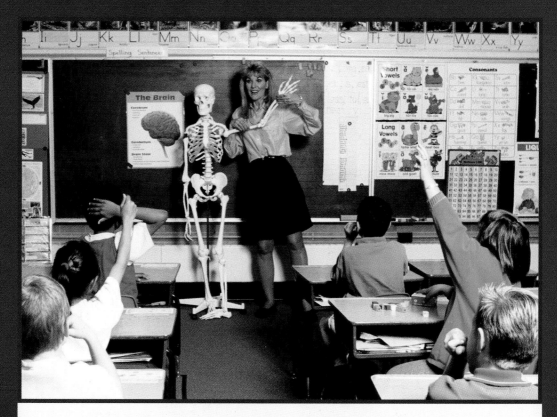

BE A WORD DETECTIVE

Can you find these words as you read about the skeletal system? Be a detective and try to figure out what they mean. You can turn to the glossary on page 46 for help.

blood vessels	marrow	skull
cartilage	nerves	spinal cord
enamel	organs	spine
joint	periosteum	tendons
ligaments	skeleton	vertebra

CHAPTER 1

THE BODY'S SUPPORT

You have bones in all parts of your body. Your bones support your body the way an umbrella's ribs support it.

Bones make up the body's skeletal system. You cannot see your bones. But you can feel them underneath your skin. You need bones to support and protect your body. Bones also help your body work.

Bones are hard and strong. Most other parts of the body are soft. Bones act like the poles inside a tent. They hold up your body and give it shape and support.

If you had no bones, you could not run, jump, or do cartwheels.

Bones and muscles work together. Muscles pull the bones to make them move. Muscles attached to your arm and leg bones help you run or throw a ball. Muscles attached to your finger bones help you write or pick up a spoon.

Bones protect organs inside your body. Your skull protects your brain. Your ribs form a cage around your heart and lungs. Your hip bones protect organs in the lower part of your body.

The muscles and bones of your hand work together to help you draw.

CHAPTER 2

Your bones help you stand up straight and tall. What is your longest bone?

WHAT IS A BONE?

Bones come in many sizes. Your smallest bone is in your ear. It is only about as big as a sesame seed. Your longest bone is in your upper leg. It is about one-fourth of your total height.

Bones come in many shapes. Long bones are found in your arms and legs. They usually have knobby ends and a straight central shaft. Short bones are found in your wrists and ankles. Your ribs, shoulder bones, breastbone, and the bones of your skull are flat bones. Bones of your spine and inner ear have odd, bumpy shapes.

The bones of your arms and legs are long bones. Bones in other parts of your body have many different shapes.

BONE SHAPES

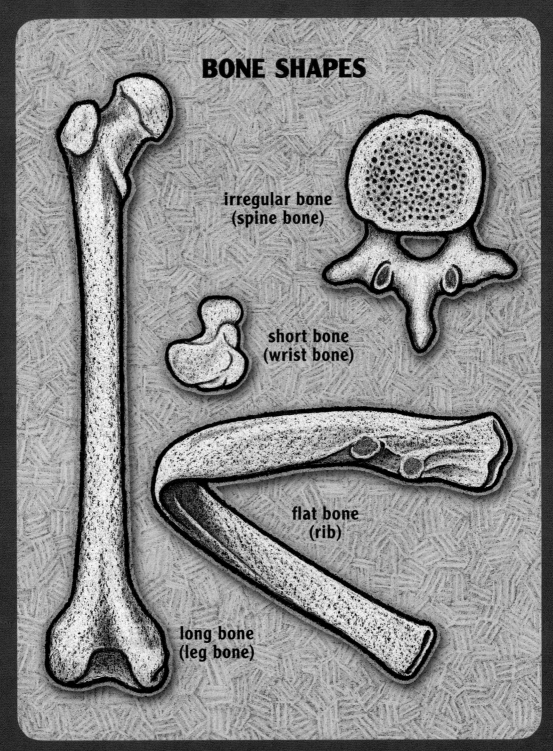

irregular bone
(spine bone)

short bone
(wrist bone)

flat bone
(rib)

long bone
(leg bone)

Most of the surface of a bone is covered with a thin layer of blood vessels and nerves. This layer is called the periosteum (PAIR-ee-OHS-tee-uhm). The periosteum helps the bone grow and repair itself.

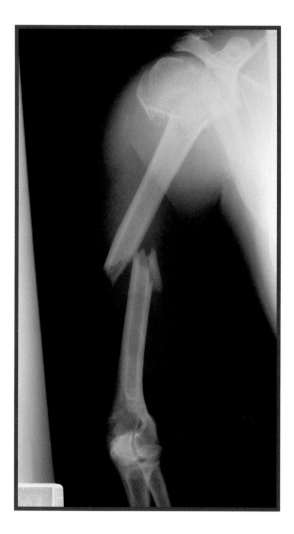

Bones are strong, but sometimes they break. This is an X-ray picture of a broken arm bone.

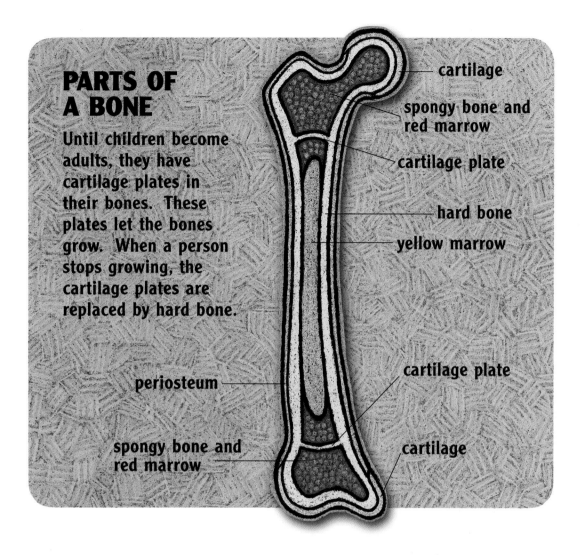

PARTS OF A BONE

Until children become adults, they have cartilage plates in their bones. These plates let the bones grow. When a person stops growing, the cartilage plates are replaced by hard bone.

cartilage

spongy bone and red marrow

cartilage plate

hard bone

yellow marrow

cartilage plate

periosteum

cartilage

spongy bone and red marrow

Beneath the periosteum is hard bone. Tiny holes in hard bone let blood vessels and nerves pass through. Under the hard bone is a layer of lighter, spongy bone. It looks something like a honeycomb.

Most bones have a soft jellylike material in the center. This material is called marrow. Yellow bone marrow stores fat. Red bone marrow makes blood cells. Your bones make thousands of new blood cells every day.

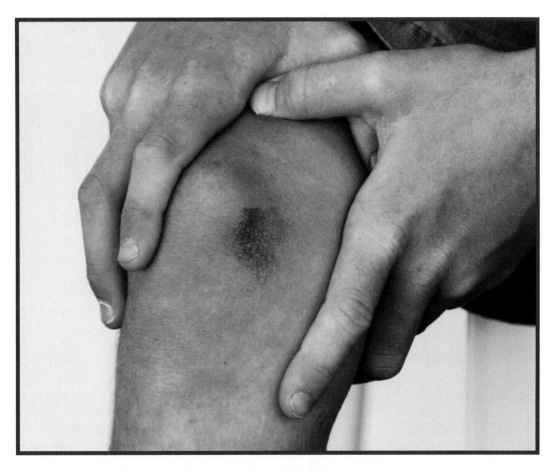

When you scrape your knee, sticky platelets in your blood form a scab to keep germs out. Platelets are made by red bone marrow.

A newborn baby's body has about 300 bones. Some of them join together as the baby grows. An adult has about 206 bones.

The ends of most bones are covered with a white material called cartilage (KAR-tuh-lihj). Cartilage protects bones where they rub against each other. You also have cartilage in your nose and ears. Cartilage is tough and slippery and can bend a little. It is not as hard as bone, but it is strong. The bones of a baby's skeleton begin as cartilage. The cartilage is slowly replaced by hard bone as the child grows.

CHAPTER 3

YOUR SKELETON

The bones of your head are called your skull. How many bones make up your skull?

Your skeleton is the framework for your body. You could not stand up or move if you did not have a skeleton.

16

The skull is at the top of the skeleton. If you touch your head, your skull feels like one big smooth bone under the skin. But it is actually 29 bones joined together. Your skull acts like a built-in helmet. It protects the organs of your head.

The top of a baby's head has soft spots. These spots are spaces between the skull bones. The spaces fill up with bone by the time a baby is about two years old.

The top of the skull covers the brain. The bones at the front of the skull support the face. Put your hands on your face. Can you feel the holes in your skull around your eyes? Your skull also has a hole for your nose and two openings for your ears.

The front of your skull has 14 bones that support your face.

This model shows what the inside of a person's ear looks like.
The three tiny ear bones are painted dark blue.

Each of your ears has three tiny bones inside. Sounds make these bones move. Nerves carry this information from your ear to your brain. Then you hear the sound.

The lower jawbone is the only part of the skull that can move. It moves up, down, and sideways. It helps you talk, bite, and chew.

Your lower jaw helps you bite into an apple.

Your baby teeth began to fall out when you were about six years old. Then permanent teeth started to grow in.

Your teeth are attached to the bones of your jaw. Teeth are even harder than bones. They are covered with a thick layer of a tough material called enamel (ih-NAM-uhl). Enamel protects your teeth from wearing down as you chew.

Your spine connects your skull to the rest of your body. The spine is a row of 33 bones. Each one is called a vertebra (VUHR-tuh-bruh). Together, they form a bony rod that supports your back.

Your back is made of hard bones. But the bones can move to let you bend over and touch your toes.

Your back twists
to let you look
back over your
shoulder.

A single bone cannot bend. But the spine
is like a row of beads on a wire. The row bends
and twists as you move. A pad of cartilage
cushions each vertebra.

The large, round part of each vertebra supports the body's weight. A hole through the center lets the spinal cord pass through. The spinal cord carries messages between the brain and other parts of the body. Muscles attach to bony spikes at the side and back of each vertebra. You can feel the knobs if you run your hand along your spine.

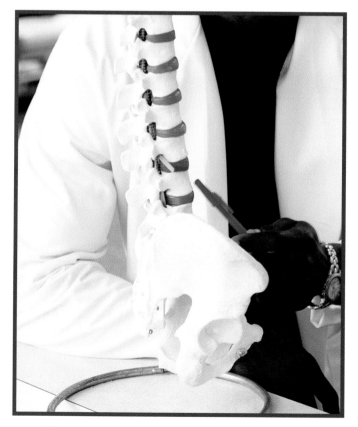

Between the bones of your back are pads of cartilage. The cartilage keeps the bones from rubbing together when you move.

Your ribs are just under the skin of your chest.

The ribs are long, flat bones curving around the chest. You have 12 sets of ribs. In the back, one end of each rib is attached to the spine. In the front of the body, all of the ribs except the bottom two pairs are attached to the breastbone. The bottom two pairs of ribs are called floating ribs.

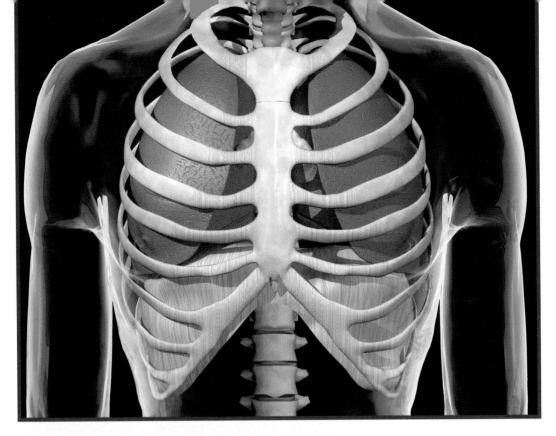

The ribs protect the organs of the upper body.

The ribs, spine, and breastbone make up
the rib cage. It is like a fence around the upper
body. The rib cage protects the heart, lungs,
kidneys, liver, and other organs.

Your rib cage also helps you breathe. When
muscles lift up your rib cage, air flows into your
lungs. When the muscles relax, air goes out.

The bones of your arm are joined to the rest of your body at your shoulder. The shoulder bone is a strong, large, flat bone in your back. In the front, the shoulder is supported by the collarbone.

The two hard bumps on your back are your shoulder bones.

Your upper arm has one long bone. Your lower arm has two bones. Hold your lower left arm with your right hand and then turn your left wrist. Can you feel the bones twist? These bones move so you can carry things or throw a ball.

Your arm bones can twist to help you swing a bat.

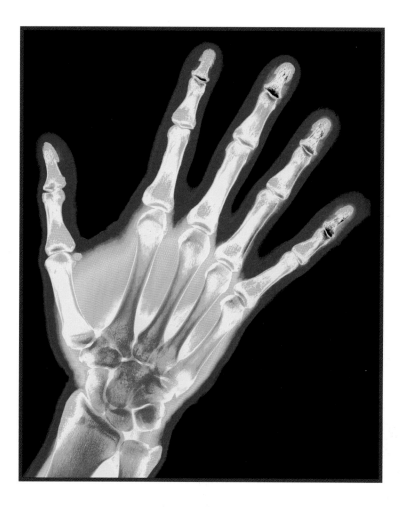

This picture shows the bones of the hand and wrist.

Your wrist is a group of small, knobby bones. These bones are connected to the five bones of your palm. Each of the palm bones is connected to the long bones of the fingers and thumb. You need your fingers and thumb to hold onto things.

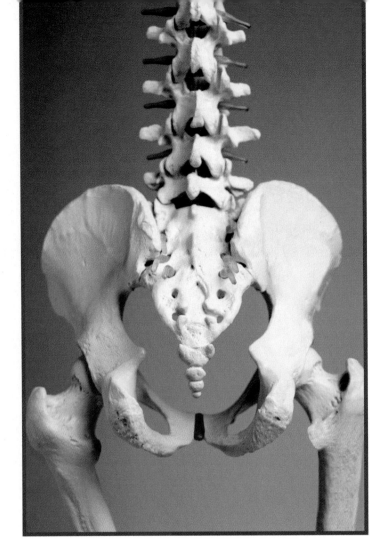

The hip bones are connected to the bottom of the spine.

The legs are connected to the rest of the body at the hips. The hip bones support the lower body and protect its organs. You can feel the top of your hip bones if you put your hand on your side just below your waist.

The upper leg has one large bone. The lower leg has two bones that can twist just like the bones of the lower arm. These bones let the lower leg turn.

Twisting leg bones let you sit cross-legged.

Do you ever fall and bump your knee?
Your knee is covered by a small bone called the
kneecap. It helps protect your knee.

When you kneel,
your knees rest on
the ground. Your
kneecaps protect
the ends of your
leg bones.

The bones of your feet are much like the bones of your hands.

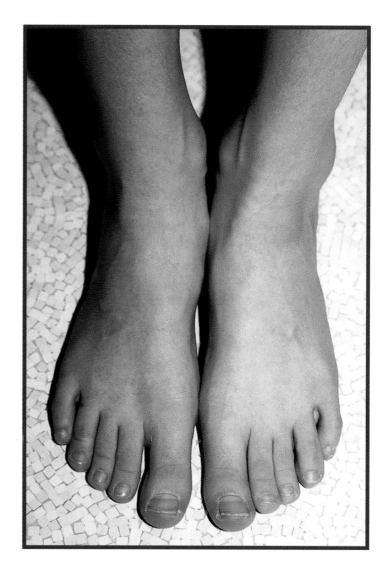

The bones of your feet are similar to the bones of your hands. But the foot bones cannot move as well. They are used mainly for standing, walking, and running.

CHAPTER 4

CONNECTING THE BONES

Bones are connected to make up the skeleton. What is the name of a place where two bones meet?

The place where two bones meet is called a joint. Different parts of the body have different kinds of joints.

34

KINDS OF MOVING JOINTS

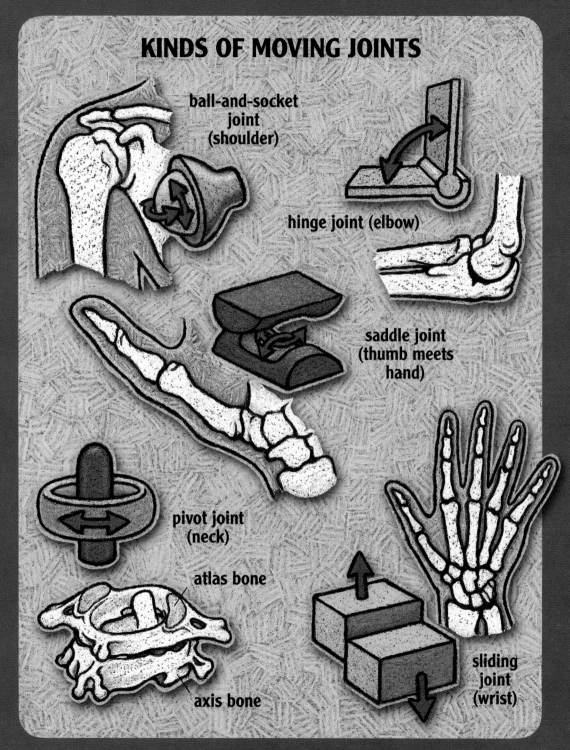

ball-and-socket joint (shoulder)

hinge joint (elbow)

saddle joint (thumb meets hand)

pivot joint (neck)

atlas bone

axis bone

sliding joint (wrist)

The ball-and-socket joint in your shoulder lets you raise your hand above your head.

Your shoulders and hips have ball-and-socket joints. The end of your arm or leg bone is round, like a ball. It fits into a cuplike shape in the shoulder bone or hip bone. Ball-and-socket joints let the arms and legs move in almost every direction.

The hinge joint in your elbow bends in only one direction.

The joints of your fingers bend in only one direction. These joints are called hinge joints. They work like the hinges on a door. You also have hinge joints in your knees and elbows.

The joint of the thumb is called a saddle joint. It is shaped like a riding saddle. This joint lets you move your thumb up and down and sideways. You also have saddle joints in your wrists and ankles.

You have a special pivot joint at the top of your spine. This joint is like a ring sitting on a peg. It lets your head move from side to side and nod up and down.

The bones of your spine are connected with gliding joints. These joints let the bones slide slightly when you bend your back. But they keep the spine stiff enough to hold up your body. You also have gliding joints in your wrists and ankles.

The pivot joint in your neck lets your head turn in many different directions.

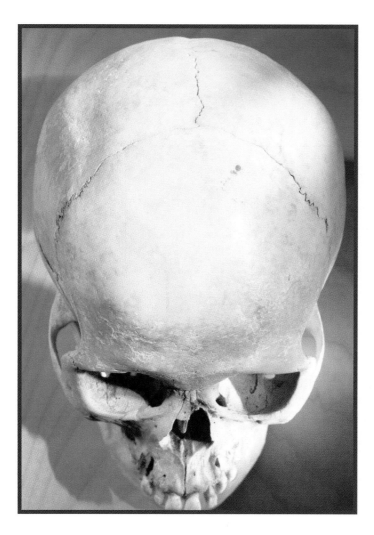

The zigzag lines on this skull are places where the different bones meet.

Some joints fasten bones together so they do not move at all. These joints are called suture joints. Your skull is held together by suture joints. They look like zigzag lines across the bone.

Muscles and bones work together.

Inside the joints that move is a liquid that helps the bones to slide easily against each other. This liquid works in the same way that oil helps a machine run smoothly.

Bones are connected with tough bands called ligaments (LIHG-uh-mehnts). Ligaments wrap around the joints and hold them together. Ligaments stretch when the bones move.

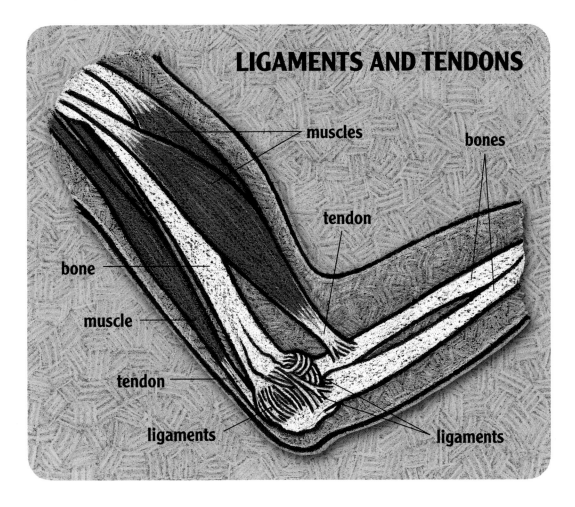

LIGAMENTS AND TENDONS

muscles

bones

tendon

bone

muscle

tendon

ligaments

ligaments

Muscles are attached to bones by narrow bands called tendons. Tendons are like strong strings at the ends of the muscles. They let the muscles pull the bones and make them move. You can see the tendons in the back of your hand move when you bend your fingers.

CHAPTER 5

HEALTHY BONES

Drinking milk helps to make your bones strong.
What other things can you do to help your bones?

Healthy bones are part of a healthy body.
You can help keep your bones strong and
healthy by eating good foods and getting
enough exercise.

Your bones need vitamins and minerals to
be strong. Milk and other dairy foods are good
sources of the vitamins and minerals bones need.

Exercise helps your bones by keeping your muscles strong. It also keeps your joints moving well.

You can take care of the bones in your back by practicing good posture. When you stand and sit up straight you avoid hurting your back.

Your skeleton is an important part of a healthy body. You couldn't stand, walk, run, or eat without it.

Exercise is good for your bones and for the rest of your body.

A NOTE TO ADULTS
ON SHARING A BOOK

When you share a book with a child, you show that reading is important. To get the most out of the experience, read in a comfortable, quiet place. Turn off the television and limit other distractions, such as telephone calls.

Be prepared to start slowly. Take turns reading parts of this book. Stop occasionally and discuss what you're reading. Talk about the photographs. If the child begins to lose interest, stop reading. When you pick up the book again, revisit the parts you have already read.

BE A VOCABULARY DETECTIVE

The word list on page 5 contains words that are important in understanding the topic of this book. Be word detectives and search for the words as you read the book together. Talk about what the words mean and how they are used in the sentence. Do any of these words have more than one meaning? You will find the words defined in a glossary on page 46.

WHAT ABOUT QUESTIONS?

Use questions to make sure the child understands the information in this book. Here are some suggestions:

What did this paragraph tell us? What does this picture show? What do you think we'll learn about next? Why do you need bones in your body? What are the different kinds of joints that connect the bones? What can you do to keep your bones healthy? What is your favorite part of the book? Why?

If the child has questions, don't hesitate to respond with questions of your own, such as: What do *you* think? Why? What is it that you don't know? If the child can't remember certain facts, turn to the index.

INTRODUCING THE INDEX

The index helps readers find information without searching through the whole book. Turn to the index on page 48. Choose an entry such as *joints* and ask the child to use the index to find out what kind of joint the shoulder is. Repeat with as many entries as you like. Ask the child to point out the differences between an index and a glossary. (The index helps readers find information, while the glossary tells readers what words mean.)

THE SKELETAL SYSTEM

BOOKS

Anderson, Karen C., and Stephen Cumbaa. *The Bones and Skeleton Gamebook.* New York : Workman Publishing Company, 1993. This book is packed with activities, quizzes, games, puzzles, and experiments exploring the human body and how it works.

Cumbaa, Stephen. *The Bones and Skeleton Book.* New York: Workman Publishing Company, 1992. This informative book about the bones and other body systems comes with an easy-to-assemble plastic skeleton model that snaps together easily.

Gray, Susan Heinrichs. *The Skeletal System.* Chanhassen, MN: Child's World, 2004. This book describes the skeletal system in a question-and-answer format.

LeVert, Suzanne. *Bones and Muscles.* New York: Benchmark Books, 2002. Learn how the bones and the muscles work together.

Maurer, Tracy. *Bones.* Vero Beach, FL: Rourke Corp., 1999. This book includes fun facts about the skeletal system.

WEBSITES

My Body
<http://www.kidshealth.org/kid/body/mybody.html>
This fun website has information on the systems of the human body, plus movies, games, and activities.

Pathfinders for Kids: The Skeletal System—The Bone Zone
<http://infozone.imcpl.org/kids_skel.htm>
This Web page has a list of resources you can use to learn more about the skeletal system.

Skeletons and Bones at Enchanted Learning
<http://www.zoomschool.com/themes/skeleton.shtml>
This site has fun skeleton crafts, plus information about the skeletons of people, birds, and dinosaurs.

GLOSSARY

blood vessels: the tubes in the body through which blood flows

cartilage (KAR-tuh-lihj): a tough, white material that protects bones where they rub against each other

enamel (ih-NAM-uhl): the tough material on the outside of teeth. Enamel protects your teeth from wearing down as you chew.

joint: a place where two bones meet

ligaments (LIHG-uh-mehnts): strong, tough bands that connect bones

marrow: a soft, jellylike material found in the center of most bones. Yellow bone marrow stores fat. Red bone marrow makes blood cells.

nerves: fibers that carry messages between the brain and the rest of the body

organs: parts of the body that have a special purpose. The heart, lungs, and eyes are organs.

periosteum (PAIR-ee-OHS-tee-uhm): a thin layer of blood vessels and nerves that covers most of the surface of a bone. The periosteum helps the bone grow and repair itself.

skeleton: the framework of bones in the body

skull: the bony case that protects the brain and other organs of the head

spinal cord: the thick cord that is found inside the spine. The spinal cord is made up of many nerves.

spine: the row of bones that runs down the center of the back; backbone

tendons: tough bands that connect muscles to bones

vertebra (VUHR-tuh-bruh): one of the 33 bones of the spine

INDEX

Pages listed in **bold** type refer to photographs.

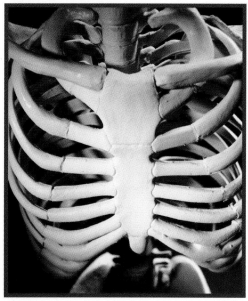